CROWD SCENES

Michael Martin

ORIGINAL WRITING

ISBN: 978-1-907179-44-0

A CIP catalogue for this book is available from the

National Library.

Published by ORIGINAL WRITING LTD, Dublin, 2009.

Printed by Cahill Printers Limited, Dublin

Acknowledgements

I wish to acknowledge and thank the following people for their support in helping me put this book together.

Mary Ryan and Jane Clarke who were my 'editorial board' and who I ran all my decisions by in putting this together. They were a good supervision group to me and I am honoured that they let me take a place where Michael used to sit with them to think and talk. They provided feedback to me in the writing of the introduction of the book.

Pat Cogan o.f.m. who put me in touch with Aoife Walsh from 'Respond!' – she gave me support and helped me find the designer of this book – Dave Manser from Vitamin Studio in Waterford. Iain Duggan o.f.m who read Michael's poetry for me and who both proof read it and gave me important comments.

Mary McEvoy and I went out one morning and took photographs of the Bull Wall – it is her photograph that is used on the cover of this book.

Garrett from Original Writing who published this book. I had help and support in being facilitated to produce what I wanted.

I want to thank everyone who has walked with me in whichever way they could since Michael died.

Dedication:

To Michael.

My name is Brid Maguire.
I am Michael Martin's wife, widow, soulmate and friend.
We were married for such a short time, nearly four years however,
I knew Michael for over 20 years.

This is the week of Michael's third anniversary.
This time of year is challenging. Feelings of absence and longing are strong these days and so also is the desire to recall and remember him. Surviving this journey of being on my own in life without Michael as my partner is something of a rollercoaster. I recall him telling me when times were exceptionally difficult that while we couldn't control what was happening to us, we could take charge of our response to these events. Publishing Michael's poetry is a response to his death. He did not have time enough to get to do this himself. While it does not change the fact of Michael's absence, I hope it leaves us with something precious from a thoughtful, special man.

Michael died unexpectedly in October 2006. He had survived an enormous battle with a benign tumour on his spinal cord in 2003. He had received a very positive prognosis as recently as March 2006. However, in June of that same year, Michael began to lose mobility in his arms and a cyst was found on the site of where his tumour had been. He underwent radiotherapy in an attempt to shrink the cyst but unfortunately this did not help. Surgery therefore, was his only option. Though initially the surgery seemed to be successful, Michael had a series of strokes while in hospital and eventually he entered a coma from which he did not recover.

Getting his poetry published was something that occupied Michael and he dreamed about this. He put many hours work into preparing this collection of 45 poems. The poems were written over many years and assembled by him in the order that they are presented. The title Michael himself chose and so my work is to bring it to fruition.

The cover of the book is a photograph of the 'bull wall' bridge in Dublin. Michael used to say that all of the major decisions of his life were made on this bridge. The significance of a bridge and especially this bridge symbolizes something of the bridging I have had to undergo in making a transition from my life with Michael to my life now. It also symbolizes the many bridges that Michael himself had to cross throughout his lifetime.

When I was trying to imagine what the cover of the book would look like I knew I was not looking for a picture of a crowd scene. I thought the emptiness of this place was an apt image which could portray the sense of release Michael experienced having written these poems. When he completed a poem it was as if he got it out of himself and then felt more peaceful. A walk on the bull wall was often his prescription for himself.

The Poems

The title of this collection of poetry is 'Crowd Scenes'. There is no poem within the collection of this name and so I was left to speculate as to how Michael found this title. Having thought a bit about this, I feel that the crowd scenes were actually the experience Michael had within himself as a poem began to emerge. He loved to find time to write but often it was as if a poem burst forth from him and he had to write. There was never a disciplined schedule for him in his writing so these poems came from him in a busy and occupying manner. There was always a rhythm and pattern after a poem was written. He would tell me that he had written a poem today. I would relish that experience. I would say "Show it to me then." "No, No, Brid. I must read it to you first and then you can look at it." Writing poems was an intensely private experience for Michael. He was shy with his work and at the same time deeply energised by it. The poem in the collection titled 'Passion' articulates something of what Michael felt when he would write. He says *the very struggle to bring the pen to the page challenges me/ unearths me/ there is a feeling and a touching and a listening that is deeper now than anything I have every known/ Somehow the struggle to write is what I am. /*

The poems themselves are largely autobiographical in content. They tell us something of the story of Michael's life and they bring us into significant moments for him. We are let into his inner world where he shows us his curiosity, his uncertainty and his deep feelings for the world he cared so much for. Some of the poems pertain to the different places he found himself in. There are poems relating to Michael's work as a priest. I think the poem 'Zagorsk' illustrates the man who ministered well.

Michael was chaplain at Dublin Institute of Technology in Dublin for some years. On one occasion he took part in a group holiday to Eastern Europe and Russia. He travelled with a group of young men who were studying apprenticeships; carpentry, plastering, welding, to name but a few.

Michael fell in love with the rich history. He loved the sounds and smells of where he was. However, he was acutely aware of the group he was with and how he needed to remember that they were having a different experience to him.

/'For now the students shuffle at the door,/
praying for the moment of my boredom/ and the return trip to Moscow
before McDonalds 'turn out the light./

Michael had an enormous capacity to be aware of what groups needed to help them move and shift and deepen their experience. His work as a group analyst was highly regarded by his peers but especially by the people who were a part of these groups.

Michael's relationship with his family was an important part of his life. His father had died when Michael was 20. A number of the poems refer to his growing up. He was the second eldest in a family of six children. Michael has two brothers and three sisters. His mother is very much alive and they all miss Michael greatly.

For Michael the question of 'Who am I' was central in his life. He pursued himself to try to understand who he was and how he had become the man he was with vigour and commitment. Michael moved from being a priest to becoming a psychotherapist and then to the life of marriage. All of these shifts were significant and Michael worked with this tension. Sometimes this journey was a struggle for him but eventually it gave him life which felt abundant and joyful. Michael entered the world of group analysis with an energy and enthusiasm which was life giving. The poem 'No orchestra' is a strong declaration of separation from son to father. The natural and healthy separating which needs to occur is expressed with humour and as always a rigourous honesty.

Michael travelled a lot. He took a trip to South Africa and Zimbabwe while he was a Franciscan and two of the poems 'Alex' and 'Africa' refer to this journey. His emotional connection to the Franciscans is captured beautifully in the relationship he had with a small group of friars who used to meet every two months to share life and offer support to each other. 'Advent afternoon in Tramore' is an affectionate and touching poem that communicates the deep bond these men felt as they spent time together.

There was always a tension for Michael in how he related to the world. He struggled particularly with his public persona and his private self. Michael was fundamentally a private man and while he came alive in company he loved the unique intimacy that developed between two people through a conversation where life and what mattered in life was being explored. Relationship was at the heart of his life. He moved from priesthood to becoming a therapist to the intimacy of marriage. I suppose at many times in his adult life he gave too much of himself away and was left feeling tired and needing to give himself care and attention. He worked with this tension and sometimes it was a struggle for him. The poem 'Silence' encapsulates this well for me.

/ I know the need to stop / to take the time to be at home/ to offer invitation to the angels on the road. /

I am pleased that in the last few years of Michael's life he did make home and the urge to overwork lessened. He loved coming to the door from work and spending time reading, cooking and chatting. Life felt easier for him.

Michael's illness and dying

I have referred to Michael's illness and death. I also need to speak something of the tremendous journey which his illness became for him, for us and for those around us. Michael and I were married a short time before he became ill. On our six month anniversary, he was given a horrendous diagnosis in Ireland which indicated his dying was imminent. Due to the resourcefulness of his family, we managed to find a surgeon who worked in America and was dealing with the problem Michael faced on a daily basis. A lot of people in Ireland made tremendous efforts to assist us in making that important journey. Michael had a successful operation to remove his tumour and while he lost some mobility he was able to return to work and our life together was able to resume. I know that what helped us both through this time was the incredible support and friendship people showed us. There was a generosity of presence and practical help which stunned us both and helped sustain us when we were both hardly able to sustain ourselves. This response to Michael continued right until his death. Michael could hardly countenance his own death, we always believed he would survive so did the people surrounding us. While there are obvious regrets with that strategy, now that Michael has gone, I do think that a necessary survival tool for him was to believe 'that all would be well'. Jane Clarke wrote a poem when Michael was in hospital in the last few weeks of his life which I feel captures well the sense and spirit of support and community which had built up around caring for Michael and me.

For Michael
by Jane Clarke

Despite the fire
of the rowan berries,
russet fountains of miscanthus,
golden glowing astilbes,
our garden is fading.

Nights grow colder
and we are waiting;
phonecalls about your eating,
emails about your sleeping,
texts about your breathing.

We rake bronze leaves,
cover dahlias with straw,
gather fallen apples.
In the waning light
we wheel one barrow after another.

Michael wrote an article for 'Spinal News' a few months before his
death. It describes in his words and in his way the experience he had
through his illness. You can read this story in the appendix.

This collection then is a legacy from Michael Martin. He was an
intelligent, thoughtful, sensitive man; a loving husband, a wonderful
friend, a loyal brother, a faithful son, a talented group analyst and a
much loved priest. No wonder then, he is so deeply missed. It is little
wonder then that I find myself struggling to come to terms with his
absence three years on.

Brid Maguire.
October 2009.

Crowd Scenes
Michael Martin

Contents

Exit	14	Saying Mass For My	
The Day After	16	Mother's Women Friends	47
Silence	18	Witness	49
Zagorsk	19	Shadow Time	50
When Will We Be Free	21	Utter Prophet	51
Did You Know	22	Hope	52
As Luck Would Have It	23	Observation	53
The Divine In The		The List	54
Barefoot Brain	25	The First Of Summer	55
Africa	26	The Meeting	56
Alex	27	Again	57
Hanging On	28	Enchantment	58
Passion	30	Gathering Courage	59
Turkeys For Christmas	31	Life	60
The Big Picture	32	Violent Men	61
Home	33	Faith	62
Abuse	34	The Big Picture	63
Time Cross	35	No Orchestra	64
The Conductor	37	Escape	65
Graham Green And Me	38	Whoosh	66
Rite Of Passage	40	Advent Afternoon In Tramore	67
One Summer In The		Triptych	68
Early Seventies	40	The Stairs	70
A Semi-Automatic Affair	43		
Poem For All Occasions	45	Appendix	72
Homesick	46		

EXIT

Into Autumn I have made
my exit
beyond the rush
to try to paint the leaves
before they die. That tree

lined exit ushers me along
whispering its years of wisdom.
The child knows
The emperor knows the child knows
But they don't know.

In this knowledge we are one

moving from proud bark to proud bark
bowing in fragile moments
of repentance
to yellow, brown and russet
webs of light.

These knarled ancestral shapes
as strong as death
as dark as light.

Now is the place of journeying
of being and letting go
windswept journeying

The mad laughter of rosy cheeks
lashed with rain
gusting

in this place of sanity

Stumbling in half dry

shoe shapes
mud of the earth, humanity.

The future fossils itself
from the splashes
we make.

THE DAY AFTER

What did you do when the yoke hurt
                    the following day?
What did you do with your new found sight
                    when you saw ?
                    After you walked,
What did you do when you stopped?
                    And did you still love,
                    after you were caught
                    loving out of turn?
What did you do with your need then ?
Did you thank your lucky stars and run ?
Were you glad to get away ?

Did you take up where you left off?
Did you cry?
Did you glance over your shoulder
to see did anyone see you
making an eejit of yourself at the well ?

There's
Nothing so exposed as being exposed
nothing so naked as being naked
nothing so real as being and knowing
                    and feeling.

ON THE DEATH OF CHILDREN

What devil's grip is this
What serpent's tongue has stung
What drunken stupor holds us
What gambling fit
What madness has begun.
>The mind is full of memories
>The heart is full of tears
>The soul a blackened shadow
>in abortive innocent years.
Lost in transient beliefs
an attempt at playing God
Living ends in death
Death carves death
and darkness reigns
amid the bullet and the bell
for there are no longer children
no children live in hell.

SILENCE

I know the need to stop
to take the time to be at home
to offer invitation
to the angles on the road.

To break bread with them
around the campfires in the desert
To the memory of Abraham
the father of letting go.
Food is the only God I know.

Cold comfort of another hunger rumbles by my side
silent with fume exhausted face
her grubby hand stark and
begging to be let inside.

Close to the fire
spoiling my chances of finding out about desire.

Caught out in my own begging years
She heaves the empty milk shake tumbler
across the cracks in the pavement
where I used to jump to escape my devil.

ZAGORSK

Onion heads the whole bus said
as we entered the northern town of Zagorsk
the centre of Russian Christianity.
"The centre of onion heads "
declared the lads getting off the bus
into lumps of ice and snow
still clinging to the corners of everything
testimony to a hard winter.
The lads thought they were bleed'en mad to live here.
Freeze the onion heads off ya they all said.

Entering the church dark like a cinema
and bright like some other place
candles flickering in the shadows
light adjusting to light
A working church
full of tourists standing round, staring at
pilgrims propped against the wall
and further down the local bodies
free of all necessity laid out
black with black shawls and brown
like the faces in Fr Browne's Connemara.

They were here before us
lying almost abandoned against the wall
their boots like the docs the students wore
scattering the floor
strange badges of identity.
Here nothing fits and everything fits
Waiting for Godot at the top of the Reek in Russia.

I long to throw myself there
into the warm romantic chant of foreign sounding prayer
to close my eyes and feel the mystery surrounding me
wondering about reincarnation
and the possibility of connecting.

These old women lighting their long tapered candles
reflecting in shadows on the bearded icons of their memory.

dancing some mad erotic dance on the incensed altar of my mind
I have been here before and the Gods have once again been kind.
Maybe...

For now the students shuffle at the door
praying for the moment of my boredom
and the return trip to Moscow
before McDonalds turn out the light

WHEN WILL WE BE FREE
(Thoughts on the day Nelson Mandela visited Dublin.)

After a week-end of freedom songs
and liberation
I cried alone
caught out on my own
Full
with the heady scent of Spring,
like a lion let loose in the sun.

The energy
let loose humanity,
On this special day of tears for men

When I ask will we be free
from the assault on our masculinity
from the baton charges of the male club
beating to pulp
the last scraps of humanity.

When I ask will the trumpet sound
and the walls come tumbling down
liberating Christ from the barren
male prison of Christianity.

DID YOU KNOW

Did you know
that people were shot in their beds
        at night ?
Did you know
        blood splattered the face
        of husband and wife ?
Did you know
        children screaming and running
        running still ?
Never again to know
        the feel of love
        of mother or father
Did you know
        mammy daddy
        daddy mammy ?
Did you know ?
        the teacher in our school
        said it was true.

AS LUCK WOULD HAVE IT

You can look but don't touch
was a phrase I picked up a few years ago
from a story told of my infant years.

An understanding nodded to intimates
and whispered to strangers
in that mouthing fashion staged
by adults for adults.

"you can look but don't touch"
became a kind of cradle song
a lullaby passed on by my grandmother
who was fond of playing cards
and superstitious about colours

It would ensure a restful night
for the second time around parents
who still hadn't a clue
and allowed aunts and uncles to play
pass the parcel with you know who.

I was born on the feast of Holy Innocence
which still summons a smile
at superficial introductions
releasing harmless associations in the mind

no one recalling

the savage destruction of children
it commemorates.
Superstition has a sharp tongue
and even longer hand

Then came the healing in the
Hawthorn bush
wild and sharp
around which the superstition grew
"You can look but don't touch"

protect the children from the thorns.
keep the bush outside
for fear of bad luck or dead cattle.

Undomesticated bush
I have no argument with you
Your story from the superstition grew.

THE DIVINE IN THE BAREFOOT BRAIN
(for John Moriarity)

It's all about too little or too much
holding on or letting go
What is is
If you want to know
But here's me walking
on the inside of a world
That on the outside isn't there anymore.

Being for the sake of not being
trying to sound intelligent
in the hope of finding
in the words, the knowledge
Or at least the searching
the feeling
The sense of me as me

No longer invisible to the naked eye
But present
   Real
Barefoot brain real
Divine even
Imagine that me.

AFRICA

Here I am white
A symbol of oppression
and a symbol of hope.
A contradiction I carry
that is neither black or white
as warm and elusive
as the air released
from two hands clapping

Here I am white
caught in the shaking dancing rhythm
of death turning to life
wailing or ululating?
that is my question
The question of the white man
who has just discovered he is white

Outside the great Zambia
barely audible in its winding flow
from rock to sand
at other times
Explodes
imitating the calling laughter of the people
in red and green and purple spurts of light

Here I am white
but I too visit the nanga in my night
and fear the touch of love that holds the mystery

of life and death
unknowning
neither black nor white.

ALEX

Somebody must have said
that you had died.
I don't know
it's like I was deaf to all that.
Or wanted to be.

The arrogance of selective hearing
is not easily detected in one so young.

Too young to feel the mantle of death
to enter the place of loss
to recognise the wounds.

Or is that just another excuse.
I signed the book,
said a mass for your soul.
A routine pious exercise I have known.

Maybe I was dead then

Walking in the graveyard
in the New South Africa
your name appears
resurrected
carved in stone.

cold and frozen
in this moment's knowing.

No longer deaf or blind or ignorant
but free to feel the shame
of my own hypocrisy laid bare
the hunger of my unfed memory
like a child I had abandoned somewhere.

"Ah laddie", what are you going to do about that ?

HANGING ON

Sometimes on Saturday mornings
I catch myself talking to books in book shops
Mumbling incoherently at this or that
knowing
to be pretentious
you have to know the alcoholic content
of every book that ever talked back.

At these times
I feel the isolation of being alone
the challenge of minding the madness

I take myself away
to a quiet table in a coffee shop
and be there

Mythical poets come and go
writing immortal lines of verse.

The dream soliloquy
has started to unravel the witches' thread
and I rock just for one unguarded moment in my chair
long enough to attract the attention of the muse
but no more

Remembering
village idiots are psychiatric cases in the city.

Stop, and the thread snaps there
worn at the thirty year mark
in the street
outside the shop
wandering home
knowing there is something I forgot
but what
It doesn't matter now for all that remains of that

Feeling again the well meaning
clatter of fear
that no son of mine would ever forget.

PASSION

The very struggle to bring the pen to the page challenges me
unearths me
leaves me feeling strangely disconnected
not touching the desk or chair or floor
not drinking the coffee in the mug I raise to my lips.

Disconnected contact

There is a feeling and a touching and a listening
that is deeper now than anything that I have ever known
Somehow the very struggle to write is what I am
on the page it flows
life formed scripted
in this still interior moment of contact.

TURKEYS FOR CHRISTMAS

Running through the sheds
we knew where to stop
and what the feeling would be.

yet we did it to scare ourselves
Forbidden fruit
has a dark whispering quality
excitement and fear lives there.

We came to stare
knowing they would soon be dead
but nobody said.

Turkeys are turkeys at the end of the day
lined up like live things
piled up squawking and screaming
under the heat of that red lamp.

We stood fascinated by their being
there. Bursting out the door
we grasped the sunlight
and left the dead to bury the dead.

Dormant
the picture in my head flicked like a switch
when someone mentioned the Beatific Vision
and I was standing there
watching those turkeys
waiting under the heat of the red lamp

the stale boredom of eternity
fixed for ever in my memory as a dead end prayer.

THE BIG PICTURE

One day before your time
you died.
In that strange way that
dying has of making you
no more.
Not gone but not huggable
either.

And I died
Something inside
connected with you,
where I had a foothold,
got a bit of who I am
died.

And then lived a bit
scared out of my wits
standing in that
big room - great hall
telling them all
I loved you.

To much
'what is'
before its time
before the place where
living and dying is no more.

Save it for me,
In our secret place.
I need to live and die a little
of the madness that we knew
before......

HOME

Here I can feel myself be
The touch of my own flesh
reminding me

of all that I have called from within
and given
and then
in that most spiritual of moments

received back again
one hundredfold
pressed down and running over.

Terrified
and giddy with excitement
knowing it is all to play for

This whole mystery
held together
by our nakedness

and dressed

for all the world to see
in all the wounds
that we have kissed.

ABUSE

The clouds that gather here
have nothing got to do with rain,
nothing as simple as a hailstorm
rumbling,

These clouds
are ordinary
dark and black.

Gloomy things
heavy
with the shock of old age

pain
that has me forever
a little stooped,
stunted

a little slow to move or speak

aware and terrified.

" I didn't know"
is caught in my throat somewhere
like a long forgotten, held back
barely remembered scream

a private aspiration

a Nuremberg prayer.

TIME CROSS
(for Adam Zagajewski)

Having arrived
I know my need to be here and
all the reasons why!

Have you felt this on your journey?

The huge market square of Rynek Glowny,
opening up its stories
telling its tale for every passerby.

I am not yet at the edge
but I have bought the canvas
and started listening to its mesmerising sound.

I married someone here a century ago
In imaginary time we travelled
just holding hands as lovers do
in the daytime.

The pigeons here are the best fed pigeons in the world.
They told me so when my hearing was as light
as the traffic-less square.

Pigeons and Lovers
Seeds and children
red and yellow blossoms
whirl in a kind of ecstasy longed for
on this journey.

Auschwitz is down the road
forever there.
I carry it within me like the worst
excesses of the Gods I have invented
to terrify my fear.

You must have known them too
in your bits of history laid bare.

Across the square
the warning sound of the trumpeter
echoes on the hour
cut short by a Tartar arrow
each death an end to time.

Like the clopping of the horses to a different beat
around the circle of the square.

And people the sky blue
wonder of their presence - free,
on holiday, smiling, writing cards
drinking beer

All enchanted by their being here.

Buying and selling
choosing and being chosen
here and now

Original Sin has something got to do with time.

The beginning and the end of all desire
of every worthwhile journey.

THE CONDUCTOR

On Vienna's Karntner Strasse
a fashionable pedestrian street
we walked - tourists
in the place to be and be seen.

Peruvian musicians play here
as in a hundred cities
throughout Europe.
Their panpipes
the familiar surround sound
of harmony
healing the humidity
drawing the largest crowds

and in the middle of the crowd
an old man - almost
a puppet
with no strings attached
conducts in full view
freely without a care.

Is he Johann, Sigmund, Amadeus
or some other Viennese memory
reminding us with every sway
of dressing up
and playing being away on holiday.

GRAHAM GREEN AND ME

The search for a character, in these streets
haunted me for a time too.
Shadows of tall towers, and even taller churches,
weeping arches
clustered beer halls, rambling market squares.

More a memory than a city
stories of love and hate.
amid the passionate intensity of war.

Distance and Hollywood
have made a fortune from my need to re-invent myself

Moving along the grey corners
the silent moody empty cafés
mysterious figures re-emerge
in overcoat and trilbies

a slight flicker of rain
Feeding my real hunger for heroes

I sense your mixture of angst and indifference
of humility and pride

Now at night
we exchange our stories
of church and state
right and wrong
east and west
communism and capitalism

North and South has yet to be invented

each holding each other's cards
and knowing the truth about our double agent status.

Ruthlessly forgiving our part in history
as actors
under the bridge or in the shadow
of the Prater ferris wheel
search for some identity
among these
bombed out autobiographical fragments.

RITE OF PASSAGE

One summer in the early seventies
before the oil crisis, I was seventeen.

Working as a helper on a lorry
for Irish Sugar Merchants
"past the five lamps
over the bridge
down to the left
just before the docks."

It had an air of mystery about it
adventure, possibility
a package deal
something out of nothing
scraps of adolescent innocence
playing along.

My Father worked there for a while
as transport manager
he got me the job
as Fathers do
in the summertime.

I was waiting for results
learning to drive his old Cortina round the yard
not like the other workers, for whom
the job was the result.
The bread and butter of my imagination
held no mystery for them.

Sitting in the canteen
trying to catch on, drinking tea
keeping my head above water
fitting in for extended moments now and then.

Laughing together about John who got nicked
walking over the bridge with bags of sugar.
"The stupid fucker
He should have flung it over."
"He was an awful eejit for getting caught
in possession"

"He was wrong anyway "
I said enthusiastically into the laughter
at once turned cold by my innocence

or worse
my being the son of the transport manager.

I remember that day I got caught
and held up for inspection
carried round the store
finally to be dumped into a hopper
full of semolina or rice or flour.

I screamed and fought and bit
then someone decided to remove my trousers
for no reason other than that.
Just for the hell of it.
My dad will hear of this I said
you'll all be sacked I said
screaming at the top of my voice.

They wouldn't bother playing any more
It wasn't any fun anyway
My sort never were.

It surfaced recently,
all eighteen years later
as an innocent spectator at a stag night.
The army were gathered at the bar.

A young man recently returned from the Lebanon
was getting married and he knew it
as they stripped him naked
and carried him through the crowd
dumping him outside the door.

He never flinched not a muscle
his naked body slumped
like a sack of flour.
A willing victim who knew the score
one of the boys
for ever more.

A SEMI-AUTOMATIC AFFAIR

"I'd like them in black and white", I said
"But it's a colour film", She said
"Oh, I know", I said, "but I'd like them in black and white"
She accepted my fixed stare and wrote my strange request on a ticket.

I had been thinking about black and white all day
about its resurrection from the dead
its rediscovery as an art form.
The shades and nuances of black and grey and light
pick out the subject in a deeper texture.
hold the memory in a different light
recognisable for its having been forgotten.

So long ago
I remember polished black shoes
and putting on my best clothes for Sunday Mass.
We all went together; a family affair.
Like the rosary at night
kneeling awkward on the ground
our arms and faces buried in the chair.
We prayed with our backs to one another
like the priest did at Mass.
We never looked each other in the eye,
A black and white exposure of a 1960s
Irish Catholic Domus Ecclesia.

John F Kennedy was shot dead in black and white
Martin Luther King was shot dead in black and white
Gandhi was stabbed to death in black and white.
All over our front room they died
black and white died
became dead old
and was consigned to a shoe box

buried
beneath everything else.

To be temporarily resuscitated
discovered by accident
on Christmas Eve
in one last demented search
for lights and baubles for the Christmas Tree.

An awkward memory fell out
there in black and white
reminding us of how we used to be.
Screams and hollers and the usual denials
"that just could not be me"!
the foolish passions for which we threw temper tantrums.
Even the 'Man from Uncle' secret identity cards.
Reminding us of how we had all been members of the secret police
secretly changing the world.

POEM FOR ALL OCCASIONS

No one could imagine that you of all people
sit there numbed to silence
by the giggling drone of tired
conversation
restlessly dumping its contents
in thick layers like Christmas pudding
reminiscent indeed

of subconscious hours
wet Sunday afternoons
stale tobacco
trips in the car,
families at war
and the football commentary is all
the memory I need.

Maybe I am mad it's not an unusual sight
head clasped in hands
brain partly submerged
partly left partly right
someone strike a balance.

HOMESICK

Of consequence so fragile
my dreams have been
the importance of every little thing.
Of leaves falling in the Borghese Garden
that first Sunday morning
Italy in full family swing.
Intimacy stretched out
within a past worth remembering
larger now than it had ever been.

Up down and up again
Homesickness has that quality
of confirming the existence
of a different place.

SAYING MASS FOR MY MOTHER'S WOMEN FRIENDS

All gathered together in the front room
arranging themselves on high backed leather chairs
and little stools
relics from the 'Year of The Pope'
"Was it '78 or '79" they chirped
like schoolgirls preparing for a midnight feast

They presided I said Mass

Everybody brought a plate
meat and bread and cakes and wine
remembering hymns from Our Ladies Sodality
for a moment they were all dressed in white
hands joined
singing the flowers of the fairest.

They presided, I said Mass

telling stories of the exploits of St. Paul
and the farewell speech of Jesus
to his disciples

Mothers their faces lined with maps of the world
where sons and daughters
came and went
leaving them, fragile in their wonder
what was all it about
where would it all end

They presided, I said mass.

Their thanks were full of praise
as we said goodnight
It was a great experience of Church
they all said
and then a clear voice cut the air
"the Church Militant " She said
As thought she couldn't
stop the words tumbling out
and they all laughed
together
like women cleaning
up the mess
as women do
making it all, alright.

WITNESS

No longer fit to stand I sit
and wonder at the purple leaves
come back to life
in the plant that died
a week ago.
Testimony to your courage
Your pain-shaped hope

I see it in your eyes
in the restaurant corner table
where an old couple silently read
the paper they used to share

the trance of making love
knowing we are barely
holding hands.

SHADOW TIME

A moody kind of evening
with firmness in its grip
Resolutions could be made
here. But there is no need

Now. All that was long ago
when evenings were occasions
to be wrestled with
knowing they would come again
to reap their harvest. Throw away the chaff,
gather the wheat into barns.
But all that is gone now too
Now that I have made the great discovery
That we only fight when there is the possibility
of a rematch.
The twilight casts no shadow
fully grown. There is only the journeys end
Coming home to all that we have known.

UTTER PROPHET

How to speak. Was that Jeremiah's dilemma
What sound to make. Not words surely
Amos, Israel
Zachary
Who gives a fig for words. Sounds

Bellowing out from Sarajavo
smoke charred groans, crushed
keening, incensed like God forsaken prayer
Graysteel. Words

sucked of all their insides
machined gunned like so much
Morse code
Rat-a-tat-tat
Communications broken down
but for the sound
Humanity gone silent
exposed in its naked force.

HOPE

Maybe it's all imagination
a kind of dreamed for longing
beyond the reach of time.
And yet it happens
that in the dead of night
I come like a thief
to the corner of my room
that keeps nix for my soul.

Imagination is the stuff
of all the possibilities selected
like priceless herbs
aromatic smells. Stillness

has a movement to it
that defies the laws of physics
exceeds the speed of light
is dark. Fermenting all

the mulch of time. Season
by season growing inside
bursting into song
silent
in the deep cavern of my soul

OBSERVATION

He let go the hope of sleeping and slept
observing his shape on the bed
held in place
in relief.

A feeling he knew from childhood
and even before that
present but absent in his mind.

Gone walkabout somewhere
in the country, by the sea
wind blowing new life
through clothes
and wisps of hair.
Held fast like a ditch in a gap
blowing mad crazy shapes
out there.

Conjuring up the man with the cap
who didn't know he was there
and the man with the cap
who did.
Both of them women in a former life
settled for raising children
from morning till night.

THE LIST

Again I make the list
of all the things that I must do
when I am not submerged in angst.
Living now the quiet white unshadowed

lie. My well worn path is safe
hungerless
the list holds everything in place.

The list becomes my reason
the thing with which I barter for my soul
like the crumpled electricity bill
in the pocket of a beggar man

I change places with on Thursdays.

Waiting for the Vincent de Paul
to means test my latest scam.

THE FIRST OF SUMMER

This is new for me too
I hear you say
In the eyes of the unwise they appeared to die
Their going a kind of give-a-way.

The body knows its own way
around the breakfast table
dropping subtle hints here and there
and great explosions
in the laughter
coming
from somewhere

still to be discovered
down the road of our childhood.

Children seeking definition
knowing it is all to play for:

the humility of not knowing
is all that sustains me

and the full moon that holds all of us
pressed down running over
giddy with the nervous wonder
of connecting.

THE MEETING

The tulips that you placed in water on Saturday
are almost fully open now,
gaping almost naked
coy frail plumage
a last concession.

Not so the wilder herbs
plucked from their beds to celebrate
the edge of pots of time
robbed of nothing
but their smell and taste and touch.

If only we who share the burden
of their mystery
could liberate so much.

AGAIN

Late morning sleep keeps me here
lucid dreaming,
the long journey over or begun

this never ending rhythm
of the dream dancing. Light
seeps through the sides
of the blue black roller blind
on the window. I am afraid

to move for fear of shattering.
Dressing but most of all
putting on my socks
these are the moments

of decision. Of shrugging off
and making my body take position.
Finding a shape to meet the day
as in pictures of doorways
I have known
with a path leading beyond.

Character precision.

ENCHANTMENT

Herbert Park in May
between the wars
faction fights
and blood letting

memories of doors
indoors, outdoors
open doors, and the other kind.
Slamming, banging
and pushing for ugly recognition.

This flower bed
an unconscious mound of clay
could have told so many stories
of awakening desire
had I known it then

If only I could breath in these
pink and yellow tulips
as Francis did the snow

Enchantment as always eludes
though passionate in its
desire to know.

GATHERING COURAGE

There is a kind of sound in the midstream
which I hear at moments
when great courage is required
to believe in my own existence.

Out there is time
a foreign friend of mine
knowing I can never know
a culture or a place
in which I have not been born or raised
in which I do not have identity
Do not speak the language.

Since I am most likely
to go first which of us will separate

Which of us will separate

LIFE

I make no apologia
to this time or space
and in return receive
no neat definition
by which to calm my fears.

I have arrived in my
basement years
and discovered the illusions
of this place

Once beautiful
with flowers and herbs
the yellow nakedness of wood
and nourishment holds out

And here another time
the dark and dreary cellar
of my cold grey bitterness
cries out

Enlightenment is here
for pilgrims of this or
any other time
the small child in me

still resists the line
"There's nothing new under the sun"
at which to pitch
my arrival and my fears.

VIOLENT MEN

"Where we come from we take the like of them and drag them
by the hair of the head to the end of the town.
Deloused, scoured down
with a good kick in the arse
too good for the like of them."

I listened to these stories again and again
all their righteousness
surrounding me, calling me
into the we powerful men.
and the one of them
that some day
I might be.

Part of the Patriarchy
the tyranny of missed opportunity and
fragility.
in the space between
we are played out
impotent now on someone else's stage.

FAITH

I have often felt this strange embrace of mystery
as real as any flesh kissed in adoration.

It is not meant to be this way
nothing sexual about the seasons
generation, the prolonged foreplay
and public consummation. Or is it

Out there for all to see
As naked as any Emperor's clothes
As full as any library of knowledge
Parchment must be kept at special temperatures
to preserve the wisdom of the ancient
text.
Though no one ever questioned
how many angels danced on the head of a pin
All agreed that God would have to be invented.

To dress the skeleton from within

In all of our religious sentiment
nakedness is our common bond.

To be present in this moment's mystery
is all
and all in this moment's mystery is present.

THE BIG PICTURE

caught up in the high church chant

the possibility of prayer
deceiving myself with an atmosphere
and hoping there might be something in it afterall

Entering the Church hushed us with its moody silence
filled with the unmistakable melody of religious music
all the chatter knocked out of us.
It was not a dark place
flickering, candles casting shadows.
mysteries blackening the ancient walls
with a feeling of history
and of something that belonged to another place.

But cold and familiar like a white washed outhouse

I imagined
Tourists standing, pilgrims propped
against the wall. Further down
the local bodies, free of all necessity

laid out black with black shawls
and brown leather beaten faces
like negatives I have seen in Fr. Browne's
Connemara. they were here before us.

Their boots like Docs scattered the floor.
Matching in that outrageous way
the student docs shuffling
as they must have done so many times
in from the April snow
Here nothing fits and everything fits
strange badges of identity,
Waiting for Godot at the top of the Reek in Russia

NO ORCHESTRA

I remember the day I told him
I had got a job as a messenger boy
for an optical company
in Pembroke Road.
It was the first summer
I would not be working in the shop
But it was more
It was a declaration of independence.
War

ESCAPE

In the beginning was the Word
and the Word was with God
and the Word was God
Hovering
not harried by time or task
contented to be
the beginning and the ending
the alpha and the omega.

Why wouldn't he, she, community be
contented by the fullness of
knowledge

Like the artist's eye on the upturned rock

freedom is the satisfaction
of anything begun and ended
seen through to the close of the plot.

WHOOSH

One word borrows another
associations in the dark
coming out to play in the daytime.

Who I am with you
is who I speak myself into.
Words are what we live by

What else......

Nothing - the gap
the uncertain destiny of it all.
Becoming, yes, no
Dare to speak, yes, no

Hearing the scream in each moment's
consummation.
Hate is a most creative force
always the tap, tap, tap
of the blind date,

the going on of this existence.

ADVENT AFTERNOON IN TRAMORE

Out from the shore
we walked all the way from the car park to the Saileens
It was a perfect walking day in late December
and we were away from it all.
Telling our stories on the incoming tide
like men walking on the water.

Just to hear the stories was enough
to know
there was hope
and the possibility of going on.
Of sharing some spark of divinity

Now in this fragment
connected as if for the first time.

Each story, its own work to do
Healing our unanswered questions
Bring us up to speed on the landscape of our journeys
Recognising all that we have done
like distant shadows blending into one
Little bits of sandy gravel sparkling in the winter sun.

'Cast your poet's eye on that', you said,
a bright fireball burning
low in the sky
Its embers warming the wisps of cloud
in the hearth of winter.

We had become the stories
that we shared
like advent mysteries unfolding
full of dangerous possibility
as naturally as dancing on the edge of that horizon.

TRIPTYCH

MORE

Imagine wanting more and getting less
setting out on a journey
with such hope,

Robbed cheated, left to die.

Not only did I not know who hit me
I didn't know I'd been hit.

Enthusiasm is a strange friend
like dependence on a passer-by.

LESS

In the morning
we shall not talk about any of this
pretend it did not happen
like the embarrassed
slip of a tongue
in a friendly kiss.

LOVE

She loves me
He loves me not
Learning the way of love
is preferable to not learning it.

Though every scrap of wisdom
is paid for
Is
in the giving in and the letting go
the saying yes and the saying no.
There is no formula, no way
We are naked
this is not a rehearsal
we are, love is.

THE STAIRS

I see you in all your dark depressing colours
bouncing up and down the stairs
Jostled and pushed along
Images of Calvary
cameras flashing
stairway to heaven
playing a long way back

memory.

I want to lead you like some demented
Pied Piper, St. Francis alla Zeffirelli
to some other place that I imagine
might be less mad.

The mud-slides of Woodstock
or even the New York Stock Exchange
cardboard boxes under Charing Cross Bridge

But you don't need to know any of this

You are holding on to
this moment's 'poster of events',
Lab books from Tom, headaches from the night before
and salvation in even the merest hint of
what might be on the paper.

'Colour isn't everything'
I hear you whisper as you let me go.

Appendix

Article for 'spinal news' written by Michael in 2006

In June 2003 I was diagnosed with a tumor in my spinal cord. For about two years I had had an irritating pain in my neck, which I thought was probably a trapped nerve or a pulled muscle. I had consulted my GP and had the usual standard x-rays but nothing showed up. Aside from taking painkillers I attended, a chiropractor an acupuncturist and one or two massage therapists. While all of these people were very caring, and I did get some relief the problem continued. In February 2003 I noticed a significant loss of power in the little finger of my right hand. My GP recommended that I see a neurologist. Unfortunately, I did not get an appointment for a couple of months, so it was June before I had an MRI scan. The MRI scan clearly identified the tumor.

While I was waiting for my appointment with the neurologist my right hand had become heavier. I thought I might have M. S. or some other muscular problem. When I was told I had a tumor I was completely shocked. For some reason the idea of a tumor had never crossed my mind. The neurologist, who gave me the news, also told me that the tumor was in my spinal cord. He told me that it was occupying the full diameter of the cord and was therefore inoperable. He there and then gave me a timeframe within which he thought I might have a chance of continuing to live. I believe that I am still quite deeply traumatised by the experience of being told within the space of about 10 to 15 minutes that I had an inoperable tumor and there was a reasonable chance I would be dead in what I considered to be a very short time.

Like many people I am inclined to think that it is the big things that change the world so this was one of those really sharp reminders that the world is a very small place where I live. My individual axis had shifted and I had no real idea what this shift meant only that it was happening and I needed to keep up to speed. Fortunately, my wife, Brid was able to be there with me at this first interview and we've been together in it ever since. It's been a real rollercoaster during which we have entered a completely different world, learnt a new language and struggled to manage feelings we never thought we had.

I spent a few days in Tallaght hospital having the diagnosis confirmed and getting more accurate MRI scans. After this I went to meet with the neurosurgeon who agreed with the diagnosis of the neurologist that the tumor was inoperable. At this stage, there was a general agreement that it was an intermedullary tumor, occupying the inside of the cord, located at a point between C1 and C3, probably an astrocytoma and probably benign. The only nice sounding word was the word benign. It should have brought some comfort but the fact that I was losing function in my right arm and was beginning to trip over my right foot, robbed it of any real solace. There was a good chance that the tumor wouldn't spread but that didn't really matter. The location of the tumor was the real problem. The neurosurgeon recommended that we do a comparison scan in about six to eight months. He expressed the firm belief that the best way forward was to do a biopsy, establish exactly what type of tumor we were dealing with and follow this up with radiotherapy. This became the biopsy radiotherapy option. The neurosurgeon, also expressed the belief that we should not do the biopsy until we absolutely had to. The biopsy was a high risk procedure, which would almost certainly result in some serious deficits.
So the plan was to give me as much time as possible with as much function as possible before the biopsy. I left the neurosurgeon with the understanding that I would only need to contact him if I experienced some paralysis. I found it difficult to understand what the difference would be between the loss of function I was experiencing at that time and something else called paralysis.

I spent the next few weeks trying to come to terms with this new world. I had two or three, panic attacks during which I really believed I was going to die. The idea of death and the feeling of being a very fragile entity in the world was truly terrifying. I have always loved life and am essentially an optimist. Like everybody I know I must die sometime, but I am in no hurry. I have lots of reasons for wanting to live, including the fact that I just love life. Brid and I began to explore all kinds of alternative ways that we might be able to deal with the tumor. While there were some very useful programs around, from diet and exercise to different kinds of visualization, all of them took time and time was not on my side. Friends and family were all working on my behalf. I got lots of useful suggestions and ideas. The problem with tumours, as I have discovered is that they are very personal, no two are alike. I had to be very clear with people that I was looking for information on how to deal with an intermedullary astrocytoma located at C1/C3 in the spinal cord. I was now aware that the condition was very rare perhaps as few as one in a million.

Then one day I got a phone call from my sister in Limerick, to say that she had read a piece in the local paper about a miracle operation to remove an intermedullary tumor. I got her to fax me the piece and sure enough, there was this story about a young girl called Aisling Riordan, who had just returned from having had surgery in Beth Israel Hospital in New York for the removal of an intermedullary tumor. Within a day or two, I had spoken with the Riordan's and had got the e-mail of Dr George Jallo. They were full of praise from Dr Jallo and expressed the conviction that their daughter would have died but for his intervention. Sadly, about a year later, Aisling did die as a result of complications, which I am afraid I still don't understand. At the time, they were full of the hope and possibility that the surgery had given them. I decided to write to Dr Jallo. I sent him a short history of my condition, and then some MRI scans. He clearly took the view that the most appropriate treatment was surgery, followed by radiotherapy, if necessary. So I now had a second option, the surgery radiotherapy option. This second option was a great deal more complicated, it could only be achieved by going to America, it was more radical, and it was expensive. Needless to say, neither option came with any guarantee. I asked Dr Jallo to send me some papers about his work, and then asked my Irish neurosurgeon what he knew of this American option. Dr Jallo sent me the paper and my Irish neurosurgeon, delivered the verdict that the American option had been around for years. It was the work of a neurosurgeon, called Freddie Epstein, it was radical, it was very experimental and it was not offering any increased life benefits. By 'life benefits' I took to mean that the awful timeframe would remain much the same.

From what I have read since I now believe that Freddie Epstein deserves at least an entire book to his amazing life. Aside from being a very inspirational neurosurgeon he is also a very inventive one. He has been trying to perfect a way of removing intermedullary tumors using what in my language is a kind of coring process. Sadly, his work was halted by a serious bicycle accident in which he suffered some damage to his brain. Dr Jallo worked with Dr Epstein, at Beth Israel, until June 2003 when he moved to John's Hopkins Hospital, Baltimore. The main thing for my search was that there appeared to be some technique here, of which as far as I could tell we had no knowledge in Ireland.

My Irish neurosurgeon had recommended that I talk to a neurosurgeon in Belfast, who had experience of working in America. I went to see this man who agreed with Dr Jallo, that surgery was probably my best option, if only for the added reason that he thought I had very little time before I would experience some significant paralysis. At this point, I learnt the disturbing information that whatever was lost in paralysis could not be retrieved in any subsequent operation. He said he would do the surgery, but I would have to accept the fact that there would be severe deficits and a very real one in four chance that I would be quadriplegic. I asked him about "motor sensory receptors". This was a piece of technology I had read about in one of Dr Jallo's papers. Apparently, this technology assisted the neurosurgeon to monitor the nerve responses during surgery and in doing so helped in the reduction of deficits. I learned that they have this technology in Belfast, but it's not very good. They have versions of it in some parts of Europe, which are better. However, according to this Belfast neurosurgeon the one in John's Hopkins is probably state-of-the-art. The danger of having the surgery in America, however, was that if I was quadriplegic I would probably not be able to come home. I wrote to Dr Jallo and he took the view that there was less chance of my being quadriplegic if I did the surgery with him. Brid and I decided to go to see Dr Jallo, before making a final decision.

It was at this stage that a number of very fortuitous events happened. I was telling a friend about my plans to go to Baltimore when he mentioned that he knew one or two people in that part of the world who might be able to help me. Through this friend I was introduced to a community of Irish Americans around the Baltimore area, to whom I will forever be grateful. Two of these extraordinary people, opened their home to Brid and I and offered us the kind of hospitality of which we could only have dreamed. Also at this time, Aer Lingus were flying direct to Baltimore for very reasonable rates.

Dr Jallo was a young upbeat matter-of-fact man who seemed very self-assured. But for me the most attractive thing about him was his experience; he was doing surgery on tumors very similar to mine every other week. On the last of our four days in American Brid and I sat down to weigh our options. We had been told that there was a good chance that radiotherapy could be effective on my kind of tumor. The problem was that the biopsy carried the same high risk as the surgery. If I was going to have the surgery there were significant advantages to having it in America. These advantages came down to three basic issues; technology (motor sensory receptor), technique (the coring procedure) and experience (Dr Jallo was doing this type of surgery on a regular basis). There were no guarantees either way, but I was only going to get one opportunity, and so we decided on surgery in America. Once the decision was made there was no point in delaying. We flew back to Ireland, having made an appointment for the surgery in three weeks time. Aside from keeping our nerve the biggest task ahead of us now, was raising the large sum of money needed before the operation could go ahead. We had an outstanding response from both friends and family. I also called in whatever goodwill I had from the past. The response was truly overwhelming. In a short time, we had enough money to pay from the operation. On a daily basis I hear about the tough cutthroat world in which we live, and yet my experience was one of enormous generosity and outstanding humanity. My health insurance was with Vhi and they did eventually come up with a large portion of the cost. My Irish neurosurgeon was particularly helpful in these negotiations with the Vhi.

However the problem at this stage was that they would not pay until we brought home the receipts and the hospital would not do the operation until we paid the money. Through the enormous generosity, of a great many people we were able to pay the bill a week before we returned to America.

We travelled out to America, two days before the operation. A friend of ours came out to stay with Brid during the difficult hours of the operation itself. The operation took about 7 1/2 hours after which I was transferred to intensive care where I spent one night in recovery. Everything seemed to go quite well except for some concern that the motor sensory receptor was not as effective as it might have been. I did not need a ventilator and on the day after the operation I was transferred to a specialist ward with other patients like myself. Dr Jallo was very positive about the operation. He felt that he had removed at least 70% of the tumor and from my present reactions hoped he had managed to avoid any serious deficits. During those first few days it was difficult to determine how successful the operation had been. I was very sore and stiff after the surgery and I remember having a lot of numbness in the little fingers of my right and left hand. Over the next three or four days I was encouraged to get out of bed and walk around the ward, and even walk up and down some steps at the end of the corridor. I had been made aware that the surgery involved an 'injury' to the spinal cord so I was very relieved when I found I could walk. After about five days, I was allowed to go home. This was partly because the people I was staying with had nursing experience but also because I seemed to be making satisfactory progress. I spent about three weeks convalescing in my new home in America. Each week, I would go to visit Johns Hopkins for some physio and follow up appointments by Dr Jallo. The stitches were removed after about a week, and I think it was around this time that I got final confirmation about the type of tumor they had removed from my cord. I was told they had some difficulty getting a conclusive identity on the tumor but that they were satisfied in the end that it was an Ependymoma. Dr Jallo made a point of telling me that if I was going to get a tumor this was probably the best type to get. I remember my Irish neurosurgeon, mentioning the possibility that it may be an ependymoma. Apparently the good thing about this type of tumor is that it generally responds well to radiotherapy. However, Dr Jallo expressed the hope that I would not need any further treatment. He had warned me that it would be several months, before I had fully

recovered from the surgery, and that during this time, I would need
to do a lot of physiotherapy. I headed home at the end of January 04,
feeling very hopeful that the worst of this terrifying ordeal was
behind me.

I contacted my Irish neurosurgeon's office the day after I returned from
America, only to be told by his secretary that he felt that there was no
need for me to see him until about two months after the surgery. I
was absolutely shocked. I was so full of my big American story that
I felt sure he would want to meet me immediately to hear about my
experience. I was also beginning to feel the first inkling of isolation.
I eventually got a telephone conversation during which I expressed
my anxiety about accessing physiotherapy. I was told that because
I had not had my surgery in an Irish Hospital I could not access
physiotherapy through the hospital system. He gave me the name of
a private physiotherapist. I contacted this woman, and got excellent
physiotherapy over the next few months. However I am at a loss to
know where the breakdown in communication took place here. Maybe
there was no breakdown in communication, and this is just the way it is
but I am amazed that things worked out this way. For the next couple
of months my time was spent travelling around the city attending
physiotherapy in one place, hydrotherapy in another and massage
therapy in yet another. This was all an expensive drain on limited
financial resources. My GP, who did see me immediately when I came
home, wrote a referral letter requesting an appointment for me with the
National Rehabilitation Hospital. Eventually, towards the end of May
I did get accepted by the NRH and attended a number of sessions of
physiotherapy, hydrotherapy and occupational therapy.

About a month after returning to Ireland I had recovered most of my
balance and was able to walk unaided. As the loss of proprioception
returned I was also able to drive. These developments were quite
exciting, and gave me a new sense of independence. However, they did
mask the extent of the deficits with which I am now struggling. It was
only when I was given a detailed examination by the OT in the NRH
that the full extent of the loss of sensory feedback in my hands became
apparent. This loss of feeling is something with which I have fought an

uphill battle for the last several months. At one level, it simply means I cannot manage any fine motor movement with my hands. But at another level, it has forced me to accept some very serious limitations, not only in what I can do, but more fundamentally, in the way I cannot do things as I used to do them before the surgery. I think it is fair to say that every step of this coming to terms with not being able has been punctuated with frustration and anger, and at times not a little despair. I know people have had to cope with far greater losses than anything I have had to put up with, so I do feel a bit guilty about my feelings.

I was very keen to get back to work, as in my mind this was an important measure of my level of recovery. I work for myself, so I had been chomping at the bit since June, but it was not until September, that I finally returned to employment. Fatigue is still a major issue, and no matter how I try it seems to creep up on me. If I do get tired it really undermines my capacity to manage the sensory deficits in my hands, and the nerve pain. I no longer attend official physiotherapy, but I have plenty of exercises to do at home. I am still taking tablets for the nerve pain, and am planning to get some nerve block injections done shortly. A great deal more has happened in these last two years then I could possibly convey in this short article. Maybe there is a level of acceptance that would help me to appreciate the richness of what I have experienced. But if there is I am not there yet. All I know is that this is my life and I want to continue to learn to live it as fully as possible.

Postscript: I wrote this article towards the end of January 06 shortly after I had had very positive results from my MRI scans. However, towards the end of March I noticed a change in my condition. I felt that there was a heaviness in my right arm and right leg. While I was hoping it was just fatigue I requested new MRI scans only to discover that the cyst portion of the tumour had expanded. After consultation with both my Irish and American neurosurgeons it seems now that radiotherapy is the best option. If the radiotherapy can target and kill the cells of the tumour then the cyst, should reduce. Physically, I have lost a lot of function in my arms and balance is very weak so I feel that I am back down at the bottom of the mountain again. I am hopeful that radiotherapy can help in this instance.

However, as I wait for my radiotherapy program to be set up I am very aware that I have to make my own happy endings, every day.

(Michael Martin is from Dublin and lives in the East Wall area. He is married to Brid and works as a psychotherapist in private practice.)